Toxicology of Substances in Relation to Major Hazards

Ammonia

M P Payne, J Delic, and R M Turner

Contents

London: HMSO

Any enquiries regarding this publication should be
addressed to the Health and Safety Executive at any
area office or to any of the following public enquiry
points:

Health and Safety Executive
Library and Information Services
Broad Lane
SHEFFIELD S3 7HQ
Telephone: (0742) 752539 Telex: 54556

Health and Safety Executive
Library and Information Services
St Hugh's House
Stanley Precinct
Trinity Road
BOOTLE
Merseyside L20 3QY
Telephone: 051-951 4381 Telex: 628235

Health and Safety Executive
Library and Information Services
Baynards House
1 Chepstow Place
Westbourne Grove
LONDON W2 4TF
Telephone: 071-221 0870 Telex: 25683

ISBN 0 11 885440 2

SUMMARY

This paper describes the 'dangerous toxic load' (DTL) for ammonia, in accordance with the principles of toxicological assessment described in the recent HSE publication *Assessment of the Toxicity of Major Hazard Substances* (1989).

The general lack of reliable quantitative human data and the variable quality of the animal studies creates uncertainty in the derivation of the DTL equation for ammonia. Nevertheless the following relationship is suggested for use in risk analyses for land-use planning applications:

$$DTL = 3.76 \times 10^8 \text{ ppm}^2 \text{ min}$$

INTRODUCTION

Since 1980 several reports deriving dose-lethality relationships for acute ammonia exposure in humans have been published[1-6]. In these reports various probit equations have been derived by using different models of the human response based upon the results of animal experiments and by making assumptions of the response distribution in the exposed population. However, none of these are considered appropriate as the basis for use by HSE in Major Hazard risk assessment, particularly for purposes of land-use planning. In consequence it was considered necessary to carry out a detailed review of the currently available data on acute toxicology of ammonia in order to determine appropriate toxicity values for use in this context.

HSE has recently published a Specialist Inspector Report describing an approach to the assessment of toxicity in relation to Major Hazards, with particular reference to the establishment of toxicity criteria for land-use planning[7]. It is this approach which is employed in the present analysis to evaluate the acute toxicity of ammonia and to derive an appropriate expression for the 'dangerous toxic load' (DTL) for ammonia. The results of studies dealing with chlorine and acrylonitrile using a similar approach have been published recently[8,9].

PHYSICAL PROPERTIES

Ammonia (NH_3) is a colourless gas with a characteristic pungent odour. Some physicochemical properties of ammonia are set out below[10,11]:

Property	Value
Molecular weight	17.03
Boiling point at 1 atm	-33.42°C
Freezing point at 1 atm	-77.74°C
Vapour pressure at 25°C	10 atm
Density at 0°C, 1atm	760 g/m^3
Conversion factor at 25°C, 1 atm	1 ppm = 0.70 mg/m^3

GENERAL TOXICOLOGICAL PROPERTIES

The principal toxic effect arising from a single exposure to ammonia gas is a marked irritation or corrosion (at high concentrations) of the eyes and the respiratory tract[11]. The remarkably high aqueous solubility of the substance results in ammonia dissolving rapidly onto moist surfaces forming strongly alkaline ammonium hydroxide which can rapidly liquefy the epithelial cells[12]. Inhaled ammonia is initially absorbed by the mucosal surfaces of the mouth, nose and throat. Destruction of the upper respiratory tract epithelium is accompanied by laryngeal oedema[13-22] which can increase in severity at least up to 48 hours post-exposure[17]. Closure of the respiratory tract by laryngeal oedema can be life-threatening in humans; this aspect of ammonia toxicity has not been well investigated in animals and it is unclear whether this effect contributed significantly to the deaths observed in animal experiments.

Sloughing of the epithelium of the upper respiratory tract can lead to blockage of small bronchi which can contribute to a fatal outcome[24,25]. Penetration of ammonia to the lower respiratory tract and lungs may produce lung damage with resultant pulmonary oedema[12,14,24,26-29]. This may subsequently result in death by bronchopneumonia and respiratory insufficiency[14,23].

In cases where medical attention has prevented death from otherwise acutely lethal exposures, lung damage has resulted in long-term respiratory deficiencies due to bronchiectasis and fibrous obliteration of small airways[17,21,28,30,31]. The voice may also be seriously affected for months or years after exposure[23,30,31]. However, there is no evidence of long-term respiratory impairment in individuals receiving exposures significantly below those producing severe, life-threatening acute effects.

In a recent report, laryngospasm was cited as an important mechanism causing death at high concentrations of ammonia independent of the duration of the exposure[1]. However, examination of the primary literature cited in support of this revealed little or no indication of laryngospasm and it is probable that this phenomenon has been confused with laryngeal oedema[13,15,17,20,22,31]. Reflex closure of the glottis accompanied by a brief loss of consciousness receding within a few seconds has been referred to[16,23]. Such a temporary interruption in breathing is a common response to irritant gases[46]. Consequently from the information available there is no evidence that 'laryngospasm' plays any significant role in the human lethal response to ammonia.

Burns to the skin may occur particularly by direct contact with ammonia liquid[12,13,15,19,27,29-33]. Severe ocular damage has followed direct exposure of the eyes to the vapour or liquid at concentrations producing severe lung damage or to ammonia in concentrated aqueous solution[12,15,34,35].

There is no evidence that ammonia is mutagenic or carcinogenic to mammals[11].

TOXICOLOGICAL DATA AVAILABLE IN HUMANS

Secondary literature sources give threshold exposure conditions for specific toxic effects in humans[12,36,37]. However these are generally revealed to be ill-founded on examination of the primary sources and therefore have not been considered further.

Experimental exposures of human volunteers have obviously been limited to relatively low concentrations. There is a wide variation of reported odour thresholds. One report gave 3.9 ppm and another about 0.70-0.77 ppm for the most sensitive of 22 subjects[38,39]. A concentration of 50 ppm for 10 minutes was moderately irritating to the skin and eyes of 4/6 subjects[40]. Following a 5 minute exposure at 135 ppm, 5/10 subjects showed signs of lachrymation and eye irritation, 7/10 had nasal irritation, 8/10 reported throat irritation and 1/10 complained of chest irritation[41]. Exposure of 7 adult male volunteers to 500 ppm for 30 minutes caused the respiratory minute volume to increase 50-250% above pre-exposure levels[42].

There are many accounts of accidental exposure to higher concentrations of ammonia but in all cases it is not possible to obtain reliable estimates of the concentrations and durations of exposure involved[12-33,43-45]. For one accident[43] the exposure was estimated to be 20 000 ppm for 30 minutes[1]. The victim died six hours after exposure.

TOXICOLOGICAL DATA AVAILABLE IN ANIMALS

Single exposure studies have been conducted in several animal species[47-64]. Studies post-1939 which resulted in mortality are summarised in Table 2. Earlier work was generally poorly conducted and reported and contributes little useful information for the purpose of this paper. Such studies have therefore not been considered further. Table 1 summarises LC_{50} values obtained from the post-1939 animal studies for various exposure times and animal species.

DERIVATION OF 'DANGEROUS TOXIC LOAD'

Estimation of exposure conditions producing the HSE land-use planning SLOT (Specified Level of Toxicity)

Useful toxicological data are available for rats and mice and to a lesser degree for rabbits and cats. There are no reliable data on the exposure conditions producing serious toxic effects in humans and no clear indications as to which of the animal species tested is the most reliable model for the likely response to ammonia exposure. In this situation we propose that the most sensitive animal species and strain should be used to represent the prediction of human responsiveness unless there are good reasons to discount such findings[7]. Although in humans laryngeal oedema may contribute to respiratory failure from the available information it is not possible to separate out this effect in deriving the DTL relationship from animal data.

From the LC_{50} values obtained for exposures of the same duration in different animal species the mouse is clearly more sensitive than the rat or rabbit (Table 1). An exception is the result of a 30 minute exposure in mice which gave an unusually high LC_{50}[58]. However this study employed a static gas exposure rather than a continuous gas stream and the actual concentration is likely to have been lower than that reported due to absorption and adsorption of the gas by body fluids, animal hair and chamber surfaces. This particular result is therefore considered to be unreliable. Studies in which the male and female animal responses were determined independently indicate a significantly greater susceptibility of male mice and rats to ammonia[53,56]. However, from the data available there is no evidence that such a sex-related difference in response occurs in humans.

In the mouse the two most sensitive responses were LC_{50} = 4230 ppm for a 1 hour exposure and LC_{50} = 10 150 ppm for a 10-minute exposure[59,54]. At this stage in the analysis, without knowing the nature of the toxic load relationship it is not possible to assess which of these two responses is the more sensitive. In both studies most deaths occurred during exposure and over 90% within 3 days post-exposure. There are no obvious grounds for considering the findings of these studies to be unreliable or unsuitable in the context of this assessment.

Derivation of dangerous toxic load equation

Only two studies, both performed in rats, have obtained LC_{50} values for several exposure periods allowing the value of n in the toxic load equation:

$$\text{toxic load} = c^n t$$

to be deduced from a linear regression of log t versus log LC_{50}[51,53]. The more recent study was specifically directed at establishing such relationships, and analysis of the data for males and females combined gave n = 2.02[53]. Although the independent n values for males and females were reported to be different in the original publication, our analysis of the data has demonstrated that this difference is not statistically significant. Analysis of the results of Prokop'eva et al gives n = 2.20[51]. However the fit of the regression line is much poorer for the data of Prokop'eva et al[51] than for those of Appleman et al[53].

Therefore, overall the results support a value for the exponent of n = 2[53]. This value has also been used in other risk assessments for ammonia releases[1,4,5,6].

Dangerous toxic load values for ammonia

On this basis (n = 2) the relative sensitivity of the above two mouse LC_{50} values may be compared. An LC_{50} of 4230 ppm for 1 hour gives a toxic load of 1.07×10^9 ppm^2 min and an LC_{50} of 10150 ppm for 10 minutes gives a toxic load of 1.03×10^9 ppm^2 min, indicating no significant differences in the sensitivity of the response in the two experiments.

The data from the animal studies giving the two most sensitive responses[54, 59] can be used to estimate 10-minute and 1-hour exposure concentrations producing a level of toxicity in mice comparable to the land-use planning SLOT. Using the method of Maximum Likelihood gives the following values: LC_1 = 6129 ppm, LC_5 = 7104 ppm for the 10-minute exposure, and LC_1 = 3296 ppm and LC_5 = 3554 ppm for the 1 hour exposure [65]. The $LC_{50}:LC_1$ ratios (1.66 and 1.28 respectively) are in both cases small indicating a steep dose-response relationship for lethality. Human variability is likely to be greater than that observed in experimental animals due to the heterogeneous nature of the human population. However since the human response is being modelled by the most sensitive animal response it is not considered appropriate to introduce a further arbitrary

factor specifically to take account of this difference[7]. Given the c^2t relationship, the LC_1 value of 6129 ppm for 10 minutes represents a more sensitive response than the LC_1 value of 3296 ppm for 1 hour (DTL values of 3.76×10^8 ppm^2 min and 6.52×10^8 ppm^2 min respectively). Consequently a suitable estimate of exposure conditions predicted to produce the land-use planning SLOT in humans is:

6129 ppm for 10 minutes.

Concentrations for other exposure times follow from the toxic load equation:

$$c^2 t = 3.76 \times 10^8 \text{ } ppm^2 \text{ min}$$

	Exposure period (min)				
	5	10	30	60	120
Atmospheric concentration (ppm)	8670	6130	3540	2500	1770

Table 1: LC_{50} values for ammonia in animals

Species	Duration of exposure	Observation period (days)	LC_{50} (ppm)	Reference
Rat	5 mins	14	26 700	51
	10 mins	14	40 300	53
	15 mins	14	17 400	51
	20 mins	14	28 590	53
	30 mins	14	10 000	51
	40 mins	14	20 300	53
	1 hour	14	11 300	51
	1 hour	14	16 600	53
	1 hour	14	7 340	52,57
	2 hours	not stated	10 920	50
	4 hours	14	2 000	49
Mouse	10 mins	10	10 150	54
	30 mins	14	21 430	58
	1 hour	14	4 230	59
	1 hour	14	4 840	52,57
	2 hours	not stated	6 310	55
Rabbit	1 hour	not stated	5 000-12 500	60

TABLE 2: SINGLE EXPOSURE INHALATION STUDIES IN ANIMALS

Species Characteristics	Exposure Conditions	Observations
Rat[48] Strain not given male and female 8 per group	1000 ppm for 16 hours	Observation period about 5 months. No deaths during exposure. One rat which died 12 hours after exposure showed pronounced lung haemorrhage but no tracheal effects were observed. The heart liver and kidneys were congested and the stomach moderately distended with a few haemorrhagic foci. No other deaths were observed.
Rat[49] Sherman male and female 100-150g 6 per group	Nominal concentration of 2000 ppm for 4 hours	A very brief report of a survey of a large number of substances. Animals were observed for 14 days post-exposure. Exposures to 2000 ppm resulted in the deaths of between 2 and 4 of the 6 rats per group.
Rat[50] 150-200g Strain, sex and size of group not given.	Concentration range not stated. Exposure period of 2 hours.	Few details given. The LC_{50} calculated using the frequency cumulation method was 10920 ppm.
Rat[51] Strain, sex and size of group not given.	Concentration range not clearly stated. Exposure periods of 5, 15, 30 and 60 minutes.	A briefly reported study with few details. Animals were observed for 14 days. The numbers of deaths for each set of exposure conditions were not stated. The following LC_{50} values were obtained:-

4

Species Characteristics	Exposure Conditions	Observations
		LC_{50} (5 min) = 26700 ppm LC_{50} (15 min) = 17400 ppm LC_{50} (30 min) = 10000 ppm LC_{50} (60 min) = 11300 ppm Toxic signs observed included dyspnoea, irritation of the eyes and respiratory tract, cyanosis of extremities and convulsion preceeding death. Exposure to a concentration of 141 ppm for 5, 15, 30 or 60 minutes produced no signs of toxicity.
Rat[52] CFE Male 200-300g	6210, 7820 and 9840 ppm for 1 hour.	The animals were observed for 14 days. The mortality results were:- 6210 ppm - 0% 7820 ppm - 80% 9840 ppm - 90% The LC_{50} with 95% confidence limits were:- 7338 (6822-7893) ppm Signs of toxicity included nasal and eye irritation and dyspnoea.
Rat[53] Wistar	Concentrations ranged from 14000-55000 ppm for 10-60 minutes.	Animals were observed for 14 days. Mortality results were:-

Species Characteristics	Exposure Conditions	Observations

10 minutes exposure:-

% Mortality

5 male and
5 female per group

	Males	Females	Combined
30000 ppm	0	0	0
33500 ppm	20	0	10
37840 ppm	100	20	60
39000 ppm	100	0	50
54200 ppm	100	80	90

20 minutes exposure:-

% Mortality

	Males	Females	Combined
26200 ppm	60	0	20
27265 ppm	20	0	10
27865 ppm	100	40	70
30690 ppm	60	60	60
33240 ppm	100	80	90

40 minutes exposure:-

% Mortality

	Males	Females	Combined
18080 ppm	40	0	30
19210 ppm	80	20	50
22740 ppm	80	20	50
23340 ppm	100	60	80
24130 ppm	100	40	70

Species Characteristics	Exposure Conditions	Observations

60 minutes exposure:-

% Mortality

	Males	Females	Combined
14140 ppm	40	20	30
14660 ppm	80	0	40
16190 ppm	100	0	50
17900 ppm	100	20	60
18970 ppm	100	40	70

Probit analysis yielded the following LC_{50} values (ppm):-

Exposure period	Males	Females	Combined
10 min	37160	45030	40300
20 min	25040	32720	28595
40 min	17560	23770	20300
60 min	14110	19730	16600

A statistically significant difference was apparent between males and females in the LC_{50} values for 20, 40 and 60 min exposures.

The data were described by the toxic load relationships:-

toxic load = $c^n t$

Species Characteristics	Exposure Conditions	Observations

where n = 1.85 for males

    n = 2.17 for females

    n = 2.02 for combined sexes.

Toxic signs seen during the exposure were eye-irritation (with eye discharge in the 60 min group), dyspnoea and nasal discharge. At necropsy all animals (including survivors) had haemorrhagic lungs.

Mouse[48]
Strain not given
male and female

1000 ppm for 16 hours.

No deaths occurred either during exposure or the subsequent observation period of 5 months.

4 per group

Animals were quiescent during exposure and no significant signs of irritation were reported.

Mouse[54]
Strain not given
male and female

8600-12700 ppm for 10 minutes

Observation period 10 days. The percentage mortality in each group after 10 days was:-

20 per group

8760 ppm - 25%

9620 ppm - 25%

10200 ppm - 55%

10770 ppm - 65%

10910 ppm - 85%

11060 ppm - 70%

11340 ppm - 55%

11920 ppm - 80%

12920 ppm - 80%

Species Characteristics	Exposure Conditions	Observations
		Probit analysis of the above data gives an LC_{50} value with 95% confidence limits of:- 10150 (9520-10580) ppm 93% of all deaths occurred during exposure. Animals exhibited excitement, immediate eye closure and irritation of the nasal passages as evidenced by pawing and scratching of the nose. Dyspnoea was evident within one minute of exposure. Death was preceded by convulsions.
Mouse[55] Strain not stated male 19-22g 20-25 per group	3590-8620 ppm for 2 hours.	A briefly reported study. Observation period not stated. Percentage mortality: 3590 ppm - 0.0% 4310 ppm - 5.0% 5020 ppm - 20.0% 5740 ppm - 40.0% 6460 ppm - 45.0% 7180 ppm - 64.0% 8900 ppm - 84.0% 8620 ppm - 100.0% The LC_{50} with 95% confidence limits calculated by probit analysis of the raw data given above is 6310 (5960-6660) ppm

Species Characteristics	Exposure Conditions	Observations
		Toxic signs included severe irritation of the eyes and the upper respiratory tract. The eyes were closed and there was a copious flow of foamy liquid from the mouth and nose, sometimes containing blood. Necropsy revealed pulmonary oedema, sub-pleural local haemorrhaging, enlargement of the heart and congestion of liver, kidneys and spleen.
Mouse[56] CR-1 male and female males 30-33g females 22-24g 10 mice per sex per group	12000 ppm for 20 min and 11000 ppm for 40 min.	Animals were observed for 48 hours post-exposure. During exposure at 12000 ppm ppm 49/53 males and 24/50 females died and at 11000 ppm 50/53 males and 36/49 females died. No further animals died in the 48 hours post-exposure. The difference between male and female mortalities was highly significant ($P \leq 0.001$).
Mouse[52] CF-1 Male 20-30g 10 per group	3600, 4550 and 5720 ppm for 1 hour	The animals were observed for 14 days. The percentage mortalities were:- 3600 ppm - 0% 4550 ppm - 30% 5720 ppm - 90% The LC_{50} value with 95% confidence limits was 4837 (4409-5305) ppm Toxic signs included eye and nasal irritation, dyspnoea and convulsions.

Species Characteristics	Exposure Conditions	Observations
Mouse[58] Swiss Albino 4 per group	Nominal concentration range of 7000-29000 ppm (static gassing) for 30 min.	Observations confined to exposure period of unstated duration. Most deaths occurred within 30 min post-exposure. No deaths occurred at exposures below concentrations of 14000 ppm. Analysis of data gives an approximate LC_{50} of 21430 ppm.
Mouse[59] ICR male 25-30g 12 per group	0-4860 ppm for 1 hour.	The animals were observed for 14 days. The following mortalities were obtained:

Experiment 1

1190 - 0/12
3950 - 3/12
4490 - 8/12

Experiment 2

1340 - 0/12
2130 - 0/12
4860 - 12/12

Experiment 3

3440 - 0/12
4220 - 5/12
4860 - 10/12

The LC_{50} derived from the pooled data with 95% confidence limits was

4230 (4070-4400) ppm

Toxic signs included tremors, ataxia, eye

Species Characteristics	Exposure Conditions	Observations
		and nose irritation, dyspnoea and excited behaviour. 95% of the mortalities occurred within 72 hours post-exposure and at the highest concentrations 90% of the deaths occurred within 15-20 minutes of exposure. In these cases irritant effects were followed by chronic seizures progressing to coma and death.
Rabbit[60] Strain and sex not stated 54 adult animals	Nominal concentration of 5000-12500 ppm (average 10000 ppm) in a static gassing chamber for 1 hour Actual concentrations would probably be lower due to absorption or adsorption to hair of animals or body fluids such as urine.	A very poorly reported study. The exposure concentration was reported to be an approximate LC_{50} based on preliminary experiments. Exposure produced increases in respiratory tract fluid, lung iron content, blood haemoglobin and plasma liquids.
Rabbit[61] New Zealand White Adult females 9 animals in experiment 1, 7 animals in experiment 2. Animals served as their own controls	50 ppm (experiment 1) or 100 ppm (experiment 2) for 150-180 minutes	Respiration rates measured during exposure and for 150-180 minutes both pre- and post-exposure. There were no deaths. Exposure to 50 ppm and 100 ppm significantly reduced ($P < 0.01$) respiration rate, by 34.0% and 32.3% respectively, compared to control conditions. No exposure related pathological changes in lungs, liver, spleen or kidneys were found.
Rabbit[62] Burgundy Tawny male 2.5Kg	1000-20000 ppm for 60 minutes on curarized rabbits.	Post-exposure period 120 min. Blood oxygen, carbon dioxide and pH were measured during and after exposure. EEG and ECG traces were also recorded. Death

Species Characteristics	Exposure Conditions	Observations
Number of animals not stated		occurred at 6000 ppm and higher concentrations. Bradycardia observed at 2500 ppm and higher concentrations.
Bat[63] California loaf-nosed bat (Macrotis californians) male and female	Nominal concentrations of 500-5500 ppm for up to 9 hours in a gassing chamber Actual concentrations may by reduced by absorption or adsorption to animals and their waste products.	No deaths were recorded at 3000 ppm. At 5500 ppm death occurred after 40 minutes exposure. Quantitative lethality data or or LC_{50} values were not given. Necropsy of bats exposed to 3500-5000 ppm before death showed large lung haemorrhages and congestion or distension of several organs notably the heart, liver and brain.
Cat[64] mixed-breed 1-5 years old 5 per group 2 untreated animals as controls for pathology comparison.	10000 ppm for 10 min in anaesthetised cats fitted with cuffed endotracheal tubes.	Animals of each group were tested for pulmonary function pre-exposure and additionally for each group 24 hours, 7 days, 21 days and 35 days post-exposure followed immediately by sacrifice and lung excision. One cat died of broncho- pneumonia on day 30 and thus only 4 were studied at day 35. 24 hours after exposure all cats exhibited severe dyspnoea and anorexia. Pathology at this time revealed necrotising bronchitis in the large airways with sloughing of the epithelium and acute inflammation. By 7 days post-exposure the mucosal lesions had healed but bronchitis, bronchiolitis and bronchopneumonia subsequently developed.

Species Characteristics	Exposure Conditions	Observations
		Studies of lung function parameters also indicated immediate and longer term phases correlating with the histopathological findings.

REFERENCES

1   Englehardt F R and Holliday M G. Dose-lethality relationships of acute exposure to anhydrous ammonia *Research report (Michael Holliday and Associates)*, Atomic Energy Control Board, Ottawa, Canada 1985.

2   Major Hazards Assessment Panel. Toxicity Working Party *Ammonia toxicity monograph.* The Institution of Chemical Engineers, London, UK 1988.

3   Eisenberg H A, Lynch C J and Breeding R J. (Enviro Control Inc). Vulnerability Model: A simulation system for assessing damage resulting from marine spills *US Coast Guard Report CG-D-137-175* available as *NTIS Report AD-A015-245*, 1975.

4   *Risk analysis of six potentially hazardous industrial objects in the Richmond area: A pilot study.* A report to the Richmond Public Authority, Dordrecht, Holland: D. Reidal Publishing Company 1982.

5   Ten Berge W F and Vis van Heemst M. Validity and accuracy of a commonly used toxicity assessment model in risk analyses. 4th Int Symp Loss Prevention and Safety Promotion in the Process Industries *I Chem E Symposium Series No 80* 11-112. The Institute of Civil Engineers, London, UK, September 1983, 11-19.

6   *Study into the risks from transportation of liquid chlorine and ammonia in the Richmond area: Selection of probit equations for acute toxic gas exposure.* Report for the Central Environmental Control Agency Richmond, Holland by Technica (Consulting Scientists and Engineers) Ltd, London, England July 1984.

7   Turner R M and Fairhurst S. Assessment of the toxicity of Major Hazard substances *HSE Specialist Inspector Report* No 21, 1989.

8   Turner R M and Fairhurst S. *Toxicology of substances in relation to major hazards: Chlorine* 1989 HMSO ISBN 0 11 885528 X

9   Turner R M and Fairhurst S. *Toxicology of substances in relation to major hazards: Acrylonitrile* 1989 HMSO ISBN 0 11 885523 9

10   Jones K. Ammonia. In: Bailar J C Jr, Emeleus H J, Nyholm R and Trotman-Dickinson A F (ed) *Comprehensive Inorganic Chemistry* New York, Pergamon Press. 1973 **2** 199-227.

11   WHO International Programme on Chemical Safety *Environmental Health Criteria 54: Ammonia* World Health Organisation, Geneva, 1986.

12   Helmers S, Top F H and Knapp L W. Ammonia injuries in agriculture *J Iowa Med Soc* 1971 **61** 271-280.

13   Slot G M J. Ammonia gas burns: an account of six cases *Lancet II* 1938 1356-1357.

14   Caplin M.   Ammonia-gas poisoning.   Forty-seven cases in a London shelter *Lancet II* 1941 95-96.

15   Levy D M, Divertie M B, Litzow T J and Henderson J W. Ammonia burns of the face and respiratory tract *J Amer Med Assoc* 1964 **190** 95-98.

16   Meythaller Von F and Gross H. Acute ammonia poisoning *Med Klim* 1957 **52** 165-166.

17   Walton M. Industrial ammonia gassing *Brit J Ind Med* 1973 **30** 76-86.

18   Dalton M L and Bricker D L. Anhydrous ammonia burns of the respiratory tract *Tox Med* 1978 **74** 51-54.

19   Hatton D V, Leach C S, Beaudet A L, Dillman R D and Di-Ferrante N. Collagen breakdown and ammonia inhalation *Arch Environ Health* 1979 **34** 83-87.

20   Montague T J and MacNeil A R. Mass-ammonia inhalation. *Chest* 1980 **77** 496-498.

21   Ward K, Murray B, Costello G P. Acute and long-term pulmonary sequelae of acute ammonia inhalation *Ir Med J* 1983 **76** 279-281.

22   White E S. A case of near fatal ammonia gas poisoning *J Occup Med* 1971 **13** 550.

23   Zygadlowski J. Acute burns with ammonia vapours *Otolaryngol Pol* 1968 **22** 773-786.

24   Derobert L. Anatomical study of four cases of acute intoxication by ammonia gas *Ann Med Leg* 1964 **44** 362.

25   Gaultier M. A summary of three cases of acute intoxication of ammonia *Ann Med Leg* 1964 **44** 357.

26   Voison C, Guerrin F, Robin H, Furen D and Wattel F. Respiratory function sequelae of intoxication by ammonia (summary of cases) *Le Poumon et le Coeur* 1970 **26** 1079-95.

27   Taplin G.V, Chopra S, Yanda R L and Elam D. Radionuclide lung-imaging procedures in the assessment of injury due to ammonia inhalation *Chest* 1976 **69** 582-586.

28   Sobonya R.   Fatal anhydrous ammonia inhalation *Human Pathol* 1977 **8** 293-299.

29   Price S K, Hughes J E, Morrison S C and Potgeiter P D. Fatal ammonia inhalation. A case report with autopsy findings *S Afric Med J* 1983 **64** 952-955.

30   Kass I, Zamel N, Dobry C A and Holzer M. Bronchiectasis following ammonia burns of the respiratory tract A review of two cases *Chest* 1972 **62** 282-285.

31   Close L G, Catlin F I and Cohn A M. Acute and chronic effects of ammonia burns on the respiratory tract. *Arch Otolaryngol* 1980 **106** 151-155.

32   Flury K E, Dines D E, Rodarte J R and Rodgers R. Airway obstruction due to inhalation of ammonia *Mayo Clin Proc* 1983 **58** 339-393.

33   Arwood R, Hammond J and Ward G G. Ammonia inhalation *J Trauma* 1985 **25** 444-447.

34   Osmond A H and Tallents C J. Ammonia attacks *Br Med J* 1968 **2** 740.

35   McGuinness R M. Ammonia in the eye *Br Med J* 1969 **1** 575.

36   Wands R C. *Patty's Industrial Hygiene and Toxicology* 3rd Edition 1981 **2B** 3045-3057.

37   Henderson Y and Haggard H W. Noxious Gases *American Chemical Society Monograph* No 35 New York, 1943.

38   Stephens E R.   Identification of odours from cattle feedstuffs *Calif Agric* 1971 **25** 10-11.

39   Saifutdinouv M M. Maximum permissible concentration of ammonia in the atmosphere *Hyg Sanit* 1966 **176** 171-175.

40   MacEwen J D, Theodore J and Vernot E H. Human exposure to EEL concentrations of monomethylhydrazine, in *Proceeding of the 1st Annual Conference on Environmental Toxicology,* 9-11 Sept 1970. AMRL-TR-70-102, 355-363. Wright-Patterson Air Force Base, Ohio, Aerospace Medical Res. Lab (1970).

41   Industrial Bio-test Laboratories Inc. Irritation threshold evaluation study with ammonia. *Report to International Institute of Ammonia Refrigeration,* Publication No. 663-03161. Cited in Ref 11.

42   Silverman L, Whittenberger J L and Muller J. Physiological response of man to ammonia in low concentrations. *J Ind Hyg Toxicol* 1949 **31** 74-78.

43   Mulder J S and Van der Zalm H O. A fatal case of ammonia poisoning *Tijdscher Soc Geneeskd* 1967 **45** 458-460.

44   Pernot C, Huriet C, Midon A and Grun G. Acute industrial ammonia intoxication A discussion of four cases *Arch Mal Prof* 1972 **33** 5-12.

45   O'Kane G.J. Inhalation of ammonia vapour A report on the management of eight patients during the acute stages *Anaesthesia* 1983 **38** 1208-1213.

46   Lindberg S, Dolata J and Mercke U. Nasal exposure to airway irritants triggers a mucociliary defense reflex in the rabbit maxillary sinus. *Acta Otolaryngol* 1987 **104** 552-560.

47   Lehmann K B. Experimental studies of important gases (Part 1 Ammonia) *Arch f Hyg* 1886 **5** 1-126.

48   Weedon F R, Hartzell A and Setterstrom C. Toxicity of ammonia and four other gases. *Contrib to Boyce Thompson Institute* 1940 **11** 475-482.

49   Carpenter C P, Smyth H F and Pozzani V C. The assay of acute vapour toxicity and the grading of interpretation of results on 96 chemical compounds *J Ind Hyg Toxicol* 1949 **31** 343-346

50   Alpatov I M. A study of gaseous ammonia toxicity *Gig Tr Prof Zabol* 1964 **2** 14-18.

51   Prokop'eva A S, Yushkov G G and Ubasheev O. Toxicological characteristics of the one-time action of ammonia on animals during brief exposure *Gig Tr Prof Zabol* 1973 **6** 56-57.

52   MacEwan, C.C., Vernot, E.N. *Toxic Hazards Research Unit Annual Technical Report.* NTIS AD-755-358, 1972.

53   Applemann L M, ten Berge W F and Reuzel P G. Acute inhalation toxicity study of ammonia in rats with variable exposure periods *Amer Ind Hyg Assn J* 1982 **43** 662-665.

54   Silver S D and McGrath F P. A comparison of acute toxicities of ethylene imine and ammonia to mice *J Ind Hyg Toxicol* 1948 **30** 7-9.

55   Alpatov I M and Michailov V I. Inquiries into gaseous ammonia toxicity *Gig Tr Prof Zabol* 1963 **12** 51-53.

56   Stupfel M, Romany F, Magnier M and Polianski J. Comparative acute toxicity in male and female mice of some air pollutants. Automobile gas, nitrogen oxides, sulphur dioxide, ozone, ammonia, carbon dioxide *C R Soc Bid* 1971 **165** 1869-1872.

57   Vernot E H, MacEwen J D, Haun C C and Kinkead E R. Acute toxicity and skin corrosion data for some organic and inorganic compounds and aqueous solutions *Toxicol Appl Pharmacol* 1977 **42** 417-423.

58   Hilado C J, Casey C J and Furst A. Effect of ammonia on Swiss Albino mice *J Comb Tox* 1977 **41** 385-388.

59   Kapeghian J C, Mincer H H, Jones A B, Verlangien A J and Water I W. Acute inhalation toxicity of ammonia in mice *Bull Environ Contam Toxicol* 1982 **29** 371-378.

60   Boyd E M, McLachlan M L and Perry W F. Experimental ammonia gas poisoning in rabbits and cats *J Ind Hyg Tox* 1944 **26** 29-34.

61   Mayan M H. and Merilan C P. Effects of ammonia inhalation on respiration rate of rabbits *J Anim Sci* 1972 **34** 448-452.

62   Richard D, Jouany J M and Boudene C. Acute 61 toxicity by pulmonary penetration of ammonia gas in the rabbit *C R Acad Sci Ser D* 1978 **287** 375-378.

63   Mitchell H A. Ammonia tolerance of the Californian leaf-nosed bat *J Mammology* 1963 **44** 543-551.

64   Dodd K T and Gross D R. Ammonia inhalation toxicity in cats: A study of acute and chronic respiratory dysfunction *Arch Environ Health* 1980 **35** 6-14.

65   Finney D I. *Probit analysis* Cambridge University Press, London, 1971.

Printed in the United Kingdom for HMSO

C25   7/90